*Throughout the volume, the two notes in this part offer alternatives:
sing the upper, lower or both as you wish.

SA(B) choir & piano

faber Young Voices

HITS FROM **The King and I** AND *Oklahoma!*

Kansas City · The surrey with the fringe
Getting to know you · I whistle a happy tune

Rodgers & Hammerstein
Arranged by Gwyn Arch

faber Young Voices

FABER **ff** MUSIC

The surrey with the fringe on top
(Oklahoma!)

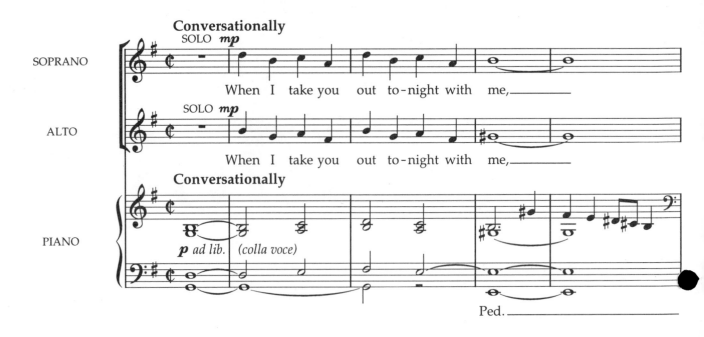

* Note: Sopranos sing this phrase only if there are no baritones.

8

Kansas City

(Oklahoma!)

Getting to know you

(The King and I)

I whistle a happy tune

(The King and I)

* Whistle, hum or 'do de do' in any octave.

faberYoungVoices *faberYoungVoices*

Two gems from 'Oklahoma!' are complemented here by timeless favourites from 'The King and I', a show which continues to hold a magical appeal for children of all ages.

The *Faber Young Voices* series is devised specifically to address the needs of young or newly-formed choirs looking for easy, yet rewarding new repertoire. Each volume offers:

- A coherent group of pieces to help with concert planning

- Arrangements or original pieces for soprano and alto voices with a manageable piano accompaniment

- An *optional* third line with a narrow range for 'baritone' (newly-changed or unstable voices) or low alto

- Excellent value for money

The series spans the fullest possible range of repertoire – both traditional and popular new material from folksongs, spirituals and calypsos to show songs and Christmas favourites.

- Faber Young Voices – the choral series for young choirs!

The Faber Young Voices series:

Broadway Classics (arr. Arch)   0 571 51660 2

Christmas Fare (Sebba)   0 571 51693 9

Classic Pop Ballads (arr. Arch)   0 571 51639 4

Favourites from 'Cats' (arr. Hare)   0 571 51614 9

Folksongs from the Wild West (arr. Arch)   0 571 51533 9

Four Jazz Spirituals (arr. Arch)   0 571 51523 1

Get on Board! Favourite Gospel Choruses (arr. Arch)   0 571 51609 2

Gospel Rock! (arr. Arch)   0 571 51638 6

Hits from 'South Pacific' and 'Carousel' (arr. Arch)   0 571 51746 3

Hits from 'The King and I' and 'Oklahoma!' (arr. Arch)   0 571 51745 5

Pat-a-pan – Favourite French Carols (arr. Arch)   0 571 51691 2

Three Caribbean Calypsos (arr. Gritton)   0 571 51527 4

'Walking in the Air' & other seasonal songs (Blake)   0 571 58047 5

West End Showstoppers (arr. Arch)   0 571 51679 3

ISBN 0-571-51745-5

Faber Music · 3 Queen Square · London

Cover design by S & M Tucker / Printed in England by Halstan & Co Ltd

9 780571 517459 >